SPOT THE DIFFERENCE

BY TAK BÙI

TUNDRA BOOKS

For my parents and Mackenzie, Leo, and Sen.

Text and illustrations copyright © 2012 by Tak Bùi

Published in Canada by Tundra Books,
75 Sherbourne Street, Toronto, Ontario M5A 2P9

Published in the United States by Tundra Books of Northern New York,
P.O. Box 1030, Plattsburgh, New York 12901

Library of Congress Control Number: 2011923471

All rights reserved. The use of any part of this publication reproduced, transmitted in any form or by any means,
electronic, mechanical, photocopying, recording, or otherwise, or stored in a retrieval system, without the prior written
consent of the publisher—or, in case of photocopying or other reprographic copying, a licence from the Canadian
Copyright Licensing Agency—is an infringement of the copyright law.

Library and Archives Canada Cataloguing in Publication

Bùi, Tak
Spot the difference / by Tak Bùi.

ISBN 978–1–77049–279–0

1. Picture puzzles—Juvenile literature. 2. Picture puzzles.
I. Title.

GV1507.P47B85   2012 j793.73   C2011–901455–6

We acknowledge the financial support of the Government of Canada through the Book Publishing Industry Development
Program (BPIDP) and that of the Government of Ontario through the Ontario Media Development Corporation's
Ontario Book Initiative. We further acknowledge the support of the Canada Council for the Arts and the Ontario Arts
Council for our publishing program.

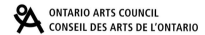

Printed and bound in China

1 2 3 4 5 6   17 16 15 14 13 12

SEEING DOUBLE? NOT EXACTLY!

If you like puzzles and problem solving, then you've come to the right place! *Spot the Difference* is a wild and crazy visual adventure that tests your powers of observation and is more fun than a barrel of . . . rabbits!

Follow the action as these energetic bunnies make music, enjoy sports, fly kites, celebrate the last day of school, hang out with friends, travel the world, explore space . . . and much, much more! *Spot the Difference* even takes you through the seasons, so you can enjoy summer in winter and visit an autumn scene in spring.

At first glance, the two pictures on each page of this book might look identical. But look again, closer this time. You'll be amazed at how many differences you can spot. In fact, there are twenty deliberate changes in each set of panels!

Spot the difference puzzles have been around for a long time and with good reason! They never lose their appeal, and they appeal to all ages. If you get stuck, you can always ask your mom and dad, grandma and grandpa, sisters or brothers, cousins or friends – you get the idea – for help. As rabbits know, the bigger the group, the more fun the challenge is. AND speaking of challenges, why not have a friendly contest to see who can find the most differences in the shortest time.

Here are some puzzle-solving hints:
- Break the puzzle into sections and carefully compare.
- Look around the edges of each puzzle.
- Check colors.
- Watch the way the wind blows or the direction of the action.
- Are there any items missing or added?
- Look at the small details, like letters or marks on clothing.
- Remember to keep count! You can make a list if it helps.

By the way, if you want to confirm your results, the answers are at the back of the book.

Good luck and hop to it!

TAK

1. SPRING THAW

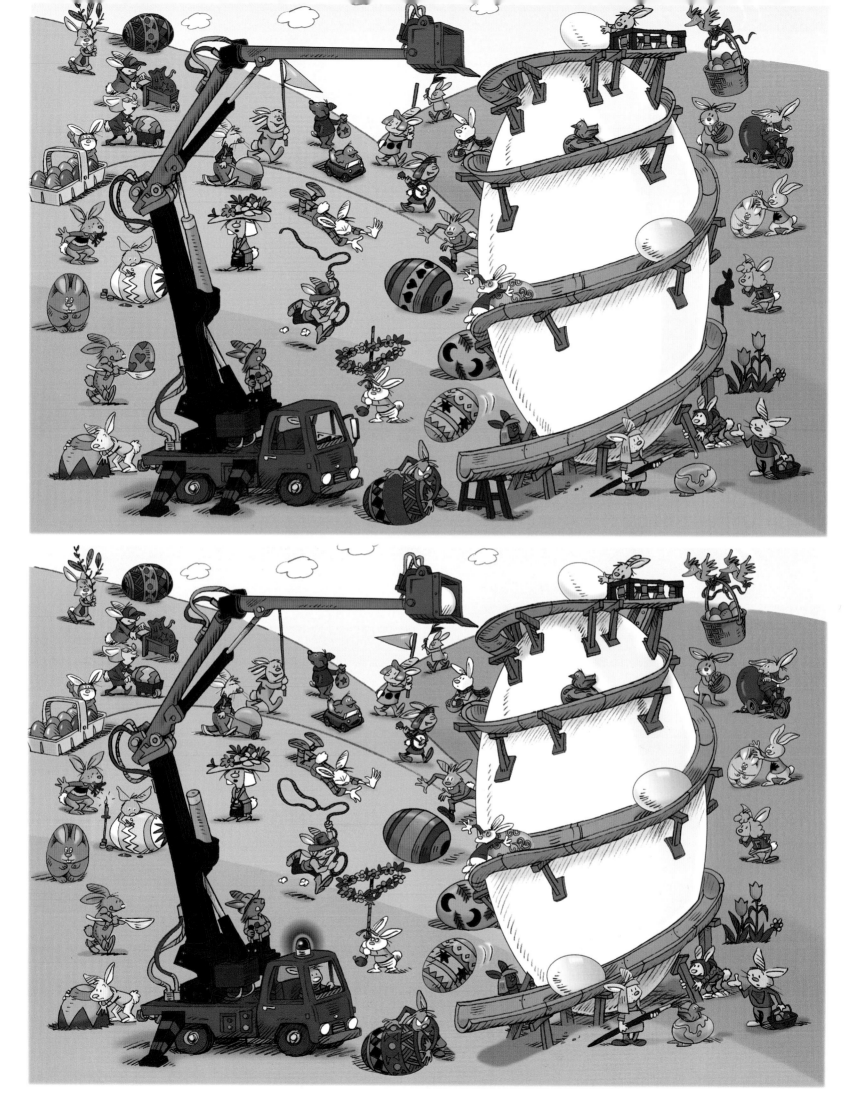

3. EGGS-CITEMENT

4. VERY, VERY VALENTINE

5. MAKING MUSIC

6. TRAFFIC JAM

7. FRESH FISHMARKET

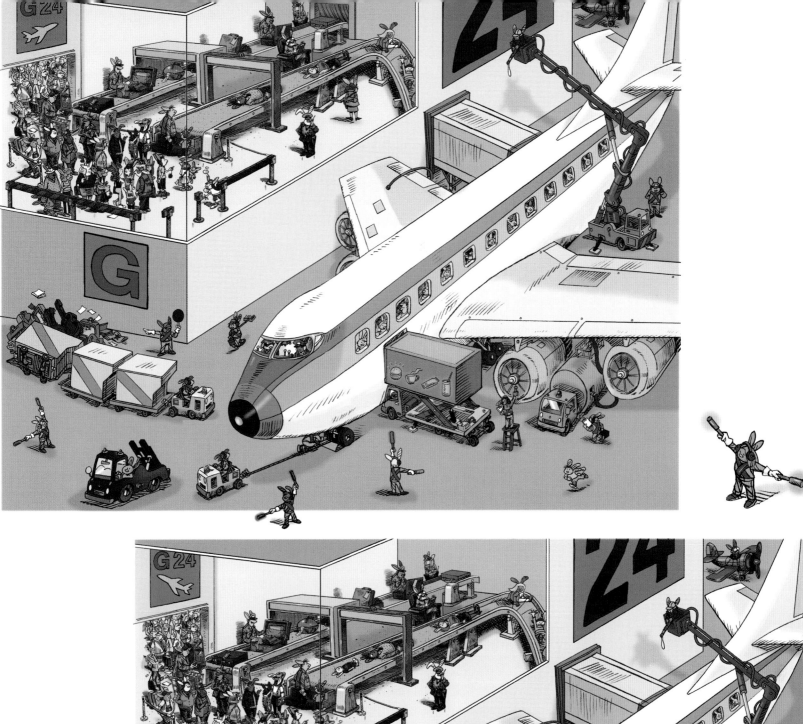

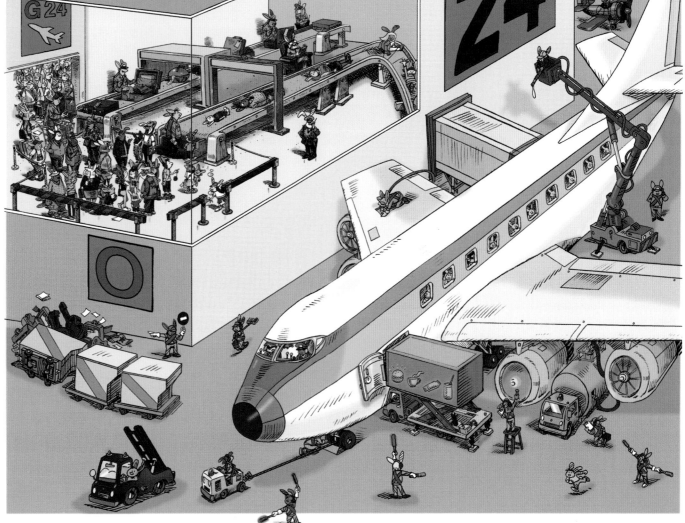

8. ACTIVE AIRPORT

9. SOMETHING FISHY

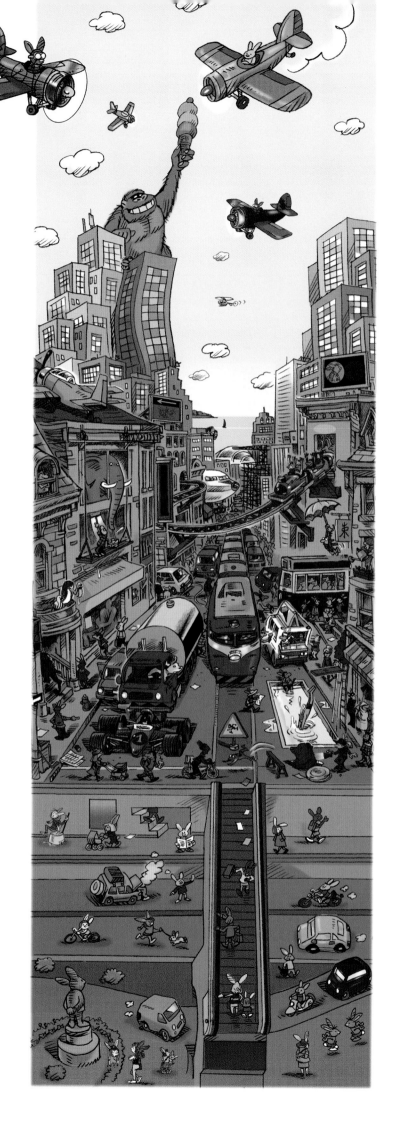

II. URBAN MYTH

13. WINTER DELIGHTS

14. TROJAN RUDOLPH

15. PENGUIN PLAY

16. ROBOT PAGEANT

17. TREASURE ISLAND

18. CARROTVILLE

19. CAMPGROUND

20. GREAT WALL

21. ROAD WORK

22. DINOSAUR DANGER

23. HAUNTED HALLOWEEN

25. SCHOOL'S OUT

27. ART SHOW

29. BEACH BASH

33. KITE CRAZE

35. RACING ROADSTERS

37. DOGS

38. CATS

39. SUMMER TRAVELS

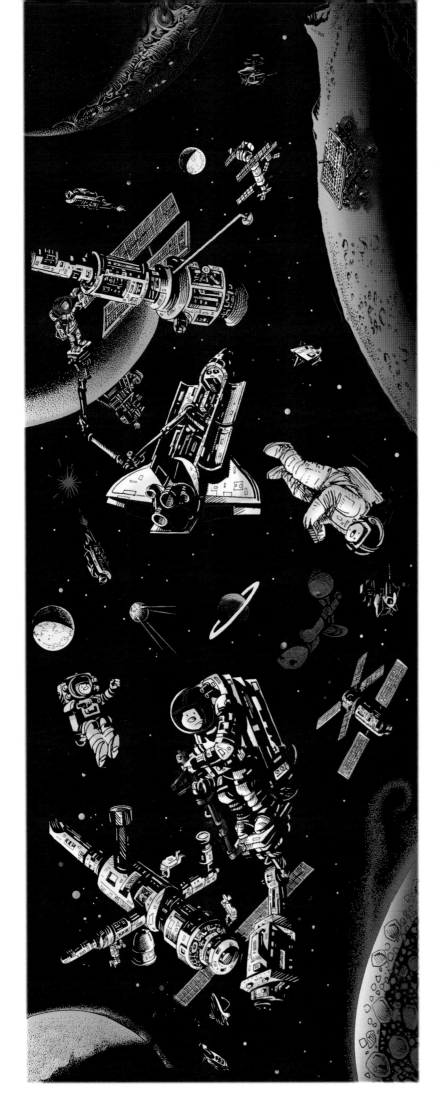 

41. THE LAST FRONTIER

PUZZLE SOLUTIONS

ALL FROM TOP TO BOTTOM, LEFT TO RIGHT

FRONT COVER

Bat-pencil is longer, pencil eraser vanishes, player is winking, only one red stripe on sleeve, logo on shirt is different, gold stripe on pants changes to red, right shoelace disappears, left shoelace is longer, right shoe cleats are gone, player's shadow appears

1. SPRING THAW

Left windmill has extra blade, cow's horns are gone, monkey's banana peel gone, donkey's tail flicked the opposite way, snowman's nose missing, extra bulrush near pond, head of swimming turtle pulled in, buoy's light cap gone, raccoon's head turned, fox tail smaller, extra headlight on tractor, beekeeper's smoke box gone, cat's tail gone, tractor's back wheel gone, handsaw blade shorter, grey duck becomes a goose, hen's comb missing, horseshoe appears on anvil, rabbit has one shorter plank, hoe's end changes shape

2. SLIPPING AND SLIDING

Top left skier loses a ski, snowboarder changes course, chimney on brick building appears, downtown building is taller, green-jacket skier loses pole, window rabbit moves upstairs, evergreen tree grows taller, snowman loses carrot nose, storefront gains a lamp, red-shirt rabbit loses curling rock, bananas appear in store window, taller chimney on house at left, gable window is closed, missing snow shovel blade, ice-fisher's catch disappears, hockey ball moves striped pole disappears, stop sign changes, kids crossing change order, green truck roof light disappears

3. EGGS-CITEMENT

Egg appears in cherry picker bucket, two bluebirds now carry basket, triangular blue flag disappears, purple flag appears, extra wood support for egg chute at center appears, candlestick at left appears, hydraulic arm missing from cherry picker, lasso appears on cowboy's rope, rolling egg at center loses hearts, rabbit at left carries empty spoon, flower garland stick is longer, chocolate bunny on right is gone, flashing light appears on truck roof, truck driver appears in cab, truck's rearview mirror disappears, extra white egg on bottom of slide, front wood support for chute disappears, chicken sits atop blue egg at bottom right, a stabilizer support for truck disappears, bottom egg has patterned green band

4. VERY, VERY VALENTINE

A spade appears on flying banner, rooftop snow shoveler disappears, chimney smoke at top right changes shape, chimney disappears from green garage, heart disappears from roof, only one second floor gable on center house, garage flag has changed, heart box gone from car trunk at left, skating rink changes shape, figure skater's legs change, red ball becomes a puck, doorknob appears on green door, star decal on window becomes a heart, garbage can is taller, shovel's blade is buried in snow at right, portrait on easel becomes a heart, dog at center bottom disappears, ladder is longer, graffiti heart on fence is larger, saw blade is wider

5. MAKING MUSIC

Added onlooker in skylight, ceiling lights are shorter, different portrait on left wall, red car on banister disappears, pumpkin appears on windowsill, cactus plant on right shelf appears, runner disappears into basement, red toy car appears on middle shelf,
mandolin head missing, dancing mouse disappears, fiddler's bow disappears, accordion player's left hand appears, mop handle appears, banjo no longer cut in half, dancing partner comes to red-jeans rabbit, slide guitar has a neck, microphone disappears, dancer girl gains cowboy hat, dance caller's finger counts one, electric cord appears at bottom right

6. TRAFFIC JAM

Green car-plane changes course, large cloud appears, yellow car-plane loses wing, red car-plane's propeller disappears, police motorcycle disappears, roadway loop disappears, car loses white camping trailer, arrow on orange truck at left changes, part of concrete road support disappears, question mark on sign becomes exclamation point, solar car at bottom left disappears, ladder on truck is shorter, window on pink truck now has one pane, minivan becomes ice-cream truck, double baby carriage becomes single, police cruiser loses roof lights, van's luggage carrier vanishes, sailboat gains a sail, statue raises its arm, racing car is flopped

7. FRESH FISHMARKET

Fish on top center blue awning is flopped, shark loses dorsal fin, awning lobster grows claws, arrow at top of escalator changes, little escalator rabbit disappears, worker's blue cap becomes red hat, shrimp sign on left wall disappears, green umbrella has shrimp logos, two salmons flip off escalator, two cups sit on umbrella table, running rabbit's net disappears, banjo player loses banjo, red fish on banner at left flops, floor sign now has an arrow, surveillance camera retracts, awning octopus has fewer tentacles, chef at bottom left disappears, dishes appear on table, clerk at bottom right appears, arrow appears on subway sign

8. ACTIVE AIRPORT

Top left departure sign changes, green baggage portal disappears, pilot added to prop plane, small rabbit added to conveyer belt, security officer disappears, broken barricade fixed, traffic director's sign changes, corner sign becomes an O, container tow truck disappears, red truck's ladder is longer, plane's nose cone changes, fewer passenger windows, plane's loading hatch vanishes, container loading vehicle loses wheels, left wing's engine is covered up, fuel technician appears on right wing, cleaner's cherry picker is shorter, cherry picker engine cab missing, traffic warden at right changes size and position, traffic warden at left changes size and position

9. SOMETHING FISHY

Bird at top is farther left, different wave at right, penguin changes direction, diver catches red crab, yellow diver's chest control panel changes, mini-sub's top fin changes, whales change, red diver now wears shoes, octopus's middle tentacle curls up, numbers on blackboard change, sun changes to star, lobster appears at blackboard, globe is blank, extra squid lies on rock, a red starfish disappears, an orange sunfish vanishes, killer whale's cheek marking disappears, extra funnel coral near bottom, pink coral at bottom right disappears, flounder fish finds a green book

10. SPRING FEVER

Big owl moves to tree house roof, added blue egg in top right nest, blue jay now on higher branch, bird feeder at left on lower branch, skylight added to tree house, one less hummingbird at right, rope ladder is shorter, step rung on tree added, blue bird on trunk faces up, wheel barrow has more soil, rabbit is higher on climbing rope, bird from bridge now on branch, kicking rabbit has red ball, blue ladder has missing rung, pitchfork is now on tree stump, hatchet moves to toadstool at right, daffodil flowers vanish, left trellis panel is missing, screwdriver lies beside toolbox, watering can disappears from pump

11. URBAN MYTH
Cloud at top left disappears, ape has extra ice-cream scoop, top right building vanishes, helicopter appears at center, ferry boat disappears, right billboard changes, plane on rooftop loses markings, rope swinger under roller coaster has purple umbrella, vulture appears on pigeon's perch, parking sign disappears, cow drives tanker truck, crocodile disappears, worker sign changes, bear climbs out of manhole, gorilla image gone from yellow poster, canoeist loses his boat, blue car moves from left side to right, broken-down car is smoking, grey van's ladder disappears, two hopping rabbits at bottom right

12. COUNTRY CAPER
Extra crane appears at top left, owl disappears, an extra cloud appears, tree branch grows longer, both birds face same direction, yellow bird loses worm, grey bird faces other way, red ant nearer tree trunk, one crow moves to back of flock, bear's foreleg changes position, tractor smoke disappears, doe disappears, car's roof rack vanishes, lamb appears near tree, extra rabbit appears, raccoon appears in tree hollow, brown mouse on fence disappears, extra bulrush appears, horse loses spots, brown rabbit appears at bottom

13. WINTER DELIGHTS
Arrow on top snowboard changed, left glove added to second snowboarder, giant snowball moves over, tallest building appears, dome building disappears, igloo builder's left arm disappears, left-side skier changes direction, street car's cable appears, street car's front sign disappears, one toboggan rider disappears, one evergreen vanishes, another snowshoe appears, fishing rod support appears, horse loses tail, skater at left wears shoes, shovel handle changes, snowman's ears disappear, hockey puck has been passed, curling stone moves left, chair moves left

14. TROJAN RUDOLPH
Santa swings on shorter rope, Rudolph's eyes close, Rudolph's nose glows, standing Santa has a hat, sitting Santa points, crawling Santa loses sack, jumping Santa loses pompom, umbrella turns green, Santa descends farther from hatch, Santa behind Rudolph's legs catches sack, motorcycle wheel becomes a ski, motorcycle's gas tank has flame decal, reclining Santa has soda can, Rudolph has extra wheel, resting Santa loses soda can, Santa dragged sack from left to right, banjo head disappears, hat now between musical Santas, Santa's arm position changes, bottom right Santa's sack shrinks

15. PENGUIN PLAY
Row 1: penguin changes direction, Emperor penguin moves flipper, rabbit on same flipper disappears, far right penguin is flopped. **Row 2:** first penguin lowers flipper, center rabbit loses blue egg, grey chick shows right flipper, King penguin's head band turns blue, last penguin's flipper folds in. **Row 3:** first penguin faces left, third penguin's head band turns orange, fourth penguin's chest loses spots, center rabbit holds clipboard, nesting penguin's crest turns red, last penguin loses neck band. **Row 4:** nesting penguin #1 trades places with rabbit, nesting penguin #2 loses flipper, fourth penguin opens beak, small penguin raises flipper, one rabbit disappears

16. ROBOT PAGEANT
Top curtain has only one layer, sign is misspelled, left robot now has antenna, rabbit's hat turns blue, both arms of yellow robot raised, third rabbit's ears disappear, third rabbit's trousers become shorts, fourth robot's crack is repaired, big robot has only one antenna, big robot's teeth disappear, big robot's control panel is lower, big robot's right arm is shorter, big robot has new red wire, another sheet of paper appears, gold trophy changes, presenter's right hand position changes, bottom right robot's funnel hat sits lower, robot's thumb changes, control buttons disappear, red oil can vanishes

17. TREASURE ISLAND
Top pirate lookout disappears, center top crow's nest is smaller, extra pirate flag appears, rope ladder attaches to middle mast, standing pirates on first mast move apart, ship's stern lamp is taller, rear pirate flag changes, only one cannon at rear, shark's fin is past pirate, second shark turns head, rowboat lamp appears, sitting gull disappears from rock, middle palm tree grows, bending pirate's umbrella turns yellow, hat disappears from sword, captain now has two pistols, treasure chest's lid is larger, pirate's pickaxe becomes a shovel, turtle swims toward shore, longer paddle in rowboat

18. CARROTVILLE
Umbrella stripes disappear, extra cloud in sky, rescue capsule is lower, extra window appears on middle building, palm tree is smaller, solar panel is smaller, roof-rabbit loses one balloon, commercial sign is shorter, carrot top is larger, theater marquee is changed, exhaust smoke floats behind carrot, white rabbit at left turns around, miner's rope is shorter, tunnel goes behind center carrot, puppy at right disappears, rabbit in yellow vest reads a letter, sitting rabbit at middle disappears, mummy disappears from cave, carrot tip disappears, green-shirt rabbit appears at bottom

19. CAMPGROUND
White cloud appears at top, the moon is flopped, campfire near tent disappears, luggage rack added to grey van, blue van disappears around the bend, hiker loses walking stick, yellow bus loses windows, canoe missing from top of orange van, green camper moves to bend above, orange striped awning changes, picnic table becomes chess table, white trailer gains door, tan trailer loses roof air conditioner, no name on pizza box, big RV gets brake lights, RV loses side mirror, RV's awning turns pink, rabbit cookie disappears at back of RV, flame gone from BBQ skewer, worm falls off fish pole hook

20. GREAT WALL
Big cloud appears at top, flag vanishes from the first look-out, second look-out has two flags, sentry disappears from third look-out, third look-out gets an entrance, flag on fourth look-out turns blue, small cloud disappears at left, knight loses his lance, fifth look-out sentry loses shield, extra cloud appears at right, the two invaders' rope is shorter, flag at sixth look-out is flopped, that look-out sentry disappears, lower invader's rope is longer, seventh look-out has two sentries, water chute is longer, surfacing rabbit at bottom disappears, carrot added to walkway, another invader added at bottom

21. ROAD WORK
Top left rabbit moves over and down, running rabbit shifts right, bulldozer's track disappears, front loader's bucket shrinks, engineering plan is blank, road sign is square, rope climber is

higher, green paver's control handles appear, tanker's top valve disappears, orange pipe becomes a carrot, sleeper under tarp is gone, hand roller becomes a wheel, soil appears in yellow dump truck, super scooper truck loses exhaust pipe, safety railing is longer, cab of dump truck changes, wood log is shorter, grey elbow-pipe appears, scope is missing from tripod, stop sign is blank

22. DINOSAUR DANGER
Horn disappears from dinosaur's head, triceratops missing spikes, brontosaurus has a head plate, center skeleton's tail turns upward, souvenir vender starts running, all toy dinosaurs disappear except one, little raptor stops running, purple dinosaur gets left forearm, its toe-claws disappear, red T-Rex loses upper teeth, left corner pup runs the opposite way, foot position of green-clad rabbit changes, roller-blades of rabbit in pink become shoes, crouching rabbit's paper towel unrolls, skateboard gets back wheels, skateboarder's shirt changes, ear of rabbit in green shirt disappears, same rabbit has more marbles, little yellow bike is not broken, rollerblader's T-shirt gains a star

23. HAUNTED HALLOWEEN
(In window display) tip of purple hat changes, devil loses middle horn, blue monster's chest emblem flopped, mummy's leg bandage tidied up, pink digital guy's mouth narrows, spider climbs higher (Outside) moon is full, bat moves left, man's newspaper disappears, house lights turn off, pirate's hat changes, his loot bag shrinks, back ghost carries two pumpkins, princess's wand has a star, iPod guy loses front dial, computer costume gains a button, chicken loses pumpkin, front ghost carries flashlight, train's smokestack is shorter, devil's trident changes

24. CRAZY CITY
Gorilla takes some bananas, streetlamp has two lights, fruit store sign changes, eagle gone from window ledge, barber pole is shorter, trash bin appears on lamp post, bear loses scarf, turtle emerging from manhole, "snow-rabbit" loses top hat, blue subway sign changes, delivery man loses parcel, cat disappears from patio, laptop appears on table, carpenter carries red tool box, yellow fire hydrant vanishes, snowmobiler reads newspaper, sitting rabbit no longer ice fishing, horse has a bridle on, red ladder is shorter, brown puppy moves down

25. SCHOOL'S OUT
Sailboat changes course, red tugboat moves to left, classroom clock disappears, red buoy moves right, parachutist swings upward, sailboat 7 loses yellow sail, blue tugboat blows smoke, hovercraft loses propellers, kite takes off, shorebird appears at left, pop can moves down, hamper moves onto dock, frog jumps past baseball player, orange ball is on shore, rowboat is farther from shore, shark-boat's cockpit closes, diving rabbit enters water, swimmer with ball disappears, submarine hatch opens, yellow camper van submerges

26. STREET JAM
Top left street sign disappears, fire hydrant is shorter, office worker loses hat, he now has a green folder, police officer holds a coffee cup, walking man's hat changes, bass player closes eyes, bongo drum loses straps, accordion changes color, only one child in stroller, newspaper gains Mona Lisa, color of man's vest changes, newspaper box window changes, yellow puppy appears, raccoon's banjo half gone, rabbit's saxophone changes, dog's trumpet is longer, man's hair piece flies off, brown puppy disappears, car has acquired sunroof

27. ART SHOW
Purple carrot flips, moon is full, light on drawing table disappears, rabbit statue holds turnip, cat mask disappears, pencil on floor disappears, silk-screen circle design vanishes, hand crank of printing press missing, vase and flower disappear from still life table, top of painting easel disappears, carrot sculpture loses stem, painter at center gains palette, sculptor loses mallet, sculpture's hole enlarges, abstract painter's T-shirt number changes, track lighting extension pole disappears, carrot sculpture's top disappears, peeking rabbit disappears, soup can changes color, bicycle fork sculpture changes

28. FARMERS' MARKET
Solar panels appear atop building, green billboard vanishes, top right cloud appears, yellow building has satellite dish, teepee behind tree disappears, bird appears in nest, dancer with pony-tail appears in line, break-dancer is flat on ground, orange awning loses stripes, cheese wheel gone from stall's countertop, juggler also tossing a carrot, sign on tree loses arrow, striped awning changes color, rabbit holds pumpkin instead of apples, hydrant appears on left sidewalk, rabbit missing from wagon, dog is closer to white rabbit, market sign's moon changes, van's roof sign changes, van's back door closes

29. BEACH BASH
Seagull is nearer to rooftop, weather flag changes, umbrella design loses fish, ball replaces book on floating raft, Frisbee player now holds ball, tennis ball becomes badminton bird, fisher now carries catch, umpire's arm changes position, his chair loses rungs, volley-ball player's hand is behind back, badminton players now use a tennis ball, bulldog's ball disappears, tablet reader now reads newspaper, red ball disappears from under white rabbit, orange Frisbee has moved right, blue and white umbrella panels change, front wheel of bike cut in half, drink cooler loses lid, red soda can moves to hamper, ice cream disappears from cone

30. ASIANTOWN
Bonsai tree blooms, bigger fish on restaurant sign, toy butterfly handle is shorter, running rabbit loses firecrackers, hydrant moves to bottom right corner, drummer's drum is smaller, other drummer now has two drums, restaurant sign loses cow logo, potted yellow sidewalk flower disappears, walking waiter carries a carrot on tray, cyclist loses paper lantern, tiger restaurant sign changes, dancing lion's tail is longer, lion has teeth in lower jaw, green lantern disappears from grocer's sign, carrots replace peppers in display bin, exiting customer gains package, brown dog disappears from road, blue aquarium fish replace crab

31. TV STUDIO
Both theater masks now laugh, top floodlight turns red, added dancer at stair bottom, camera appears at right, number 3 camera becomes number 6, more cables show up at left, clapboard snaps shut, microphone disappears, tree prop sits directly on floor, number 2 camera loses lens hood, fire extinguisher disappears, neck of bass is longer, third sheet of piano music appears, sheet music appears in front of flautist, top second left monitor changes color, knobs disappear from left desk, wall switch appears, straw disappears from drink, coffee mug vanishes

32. IF THE SHOE FITS . . .
Strap changes on top shoe, rabbit holding tulips slips down, window appears on wooden clog, lace changes on blue shoe, extra log support on hillside, brown boot loses chimney, its roof has skylight, one of its windows disappears, hanging sock becomes a

towel, clothespin disappears from sock, clothesline support thinner, sitting rabbit now plays guitar, leaves appear on tree at left, computer gone from running shoe, shoelace is longer, entrance door changes, hydrant disappears, car's hatchback disappears, design on truck's side changes, rabbit's lunch disappears

33. KITE CRAZE

Little blue kite loses tail, rectangular kite moves left, triangular kite replaces it, dragon kite's tail is longer, box kite is shorter, fish kite loses tailfin, monk kite's wing position changes, butterfly kite is smaller, moth kite vanishes, bluebird kite's wings grow, gargoyle face disappears, window panes appear on left temple, bat kite loses ears, rabbit with kite appears on balcony, green kite changes direction, bamboo fence near bridge is lower, dog with string ball moves to bottom right, large kite with wave design changes, rabbit at center bottom loses kite, kite on ground changes design

34. AIRCRAFT CARRIER

Jet's nose antenna disappears, jet gains second exhaust port, jet's tail flaps are yellow, planet decal on tailfin disappears, jet's landing gear retracts, shorter rescue cable on chopper, blue plane's landing gear is down, twin engine chopper has smaller load, yellow chopper loses patient, landing plane loses tail hook, green chopper now has wheels, blue chopper's tail rotor is working, flag design changes, letter V changes to letter A, arrow added to mid-deck, sailor's fishing rod disappears, signaling rabbit disappears, landing target rotates, deck number is now 15, left propeller disappears from blue plane

35. RACING ROADSTERS

Camper van loses roof, blue motorcycle moves forward, top flag turns green, old blue car #9 moves back, red traffic cone appears, second flag turns yellow, blue car's number changes to 66, tire changer vanishes, driver missing from motorcycle with sidecar, second traffic cone moves, car 90 loses front tire, car 5 moves forward, tow truck's hook disappears, blue formula car loses spoiler, same car loses front stabilizer, buggy racer 9 moves to center lane, pink scooter 6 moves to right, flagman's podium disappears, red formula car's number changes, motorcycle 8 wins

36. UNDER THE BIG TOP

First spotlight turns blue, blue flag appears on tent, bird disappears, mauve stripe turns orange, trapeze artist moves closer to catcher, pyramid's top rabbit costume changes, giant rabbit's eyes close, ball at left is inside ring, ball moves outside ring at right, yellow clown disappears, orange horse turns, airborne tumbler vanishes, ring master's arm position changes, magician pulls rabbit from hat, jumping rabbit is closer to hoop, shovel at right disappears, clown car at left disappears, top half of hoop disappears, ring master's arm changes, vendor's left hand holds carrot snack

37. DOGS

Bloodhound has spots, dachshund's body is longer, mountain dog's tail curls, its paws are now brown, bulldog has a tail, small hound faces other way, bowing dog's tail is curlier, rabbit's jacket turns red, his cat disappears, chihuahua trades place with Westie, poodle loses pompom, hound gains more brown patches, its ears pop up, dalmatian loses many spots, rabbit's ears vanish, brown dachshund has light chest and belly, fox terrier loses dark saddle patch, French bulldog acquires patches, bottom rabbit's ears are straight, grey dog acquires dark stripes

38. CATS

Catmobile carries extra sitting passenger, its ears turn, its nose moves down, its driver disappears, dark brown and white cat has whiskers, mouse escapes from tailless cat, striped cat's tail is straight, Siamese cat loses spots, dancing cat's hat is smaller, happy cat now holds mouse, basset hound has dark patch, hitch hiker's sign changes direction, boat rudder is smaller, hairless cat loses markings, cat's letter changes color, cat actor loses skull, reclining cat's tail shrinks, cricket bat becomes baseball bat, fishbowl upside down, tiger cat loses head stripes

39. SUMMER TRAVELS

Rabbit comes out of tent, bear cub disappears, red car carries added canoe, bird with twig moves to middle right side, lookout tower gains a roof, plane loses both wing floats, bulrushes at left disappear, lighthouse grows taller, tent turns blue, campfire is out, hang glider turns red, cow's tail disappears, small hang glider changes color, horse loses buggy, giant bird's wing turns blue, fishing boat loses pole, tugboat changes direction, speed boat moves left, buoy moves right and up, ferry emits more smoke

40. BACK TO SCHOOL

Squirrel goes opposite way, colors change on flag, raccoon moves out of nest, time changes on clock, blackboard numbers change, globe has holding bracket, desk and chair disappear from classroom, apple disappears from front desk, rooster's comb disappears, another bunch of red berries hang at right, tower loses antenna, teacher near doorway rings a bell, lady teacher's clipboard disappears, yellow bird at right vanishes, student's yo-yo string is shorter, student at left carries lunch box, crouching student picks up book, yellow rabbit at bottom acquires back-pack, rabbit hiding under log disappears, log is no longer hollow

41. THE LAST FRONTIER

Surface probe vehicle near top right has extra wheel, its antenna is taller, large satellite at left loses solar panel, repairing astronaut (gold helmet) moves farther up, satellite probe is shorter, another exhaust appears, purple-helmet astronaut's backpack is larger, shuttle's two front roof panels disappear, two of shuttle's wing flaps disappear, shuttle gains a rear engine, blue moon at left is more full, nearby satellite changes direction, Saturn's ring vanishes, orange spacecraft has extra pod, brown astronaut's holds repair kit, red-helmet astronaut holds a camera, his standing platform extension appears, space station's bottom solar panel grows, purple planet has raised surfaces, heat flare disappears from gold planet